Original title:
Echoes of the Eucalyptus

Copyright © 2025 Creative Arts Management OÜ
All rights reserved.

Author: Eleanor Prescott
ISBN HARDBACK: 978-1-80567-182-4
ISBN PAPERBACK: 978-1-80567-481-8

## Murmurs of the Forest Floor

Beneath the trees, critters creep,
Squirrels debate their nutty heap.
A deer trips over its own two feet,
While mushrooms giggle, oh what a feat!

Frogs in a band, they set the tone,
Ribbiting rhythms, on their own throne.
A fox sings opera, rather quite loud,
The audience giggles, not at all cowed.

## Shadows in the Grove

In the shade, a raccoon prances,
Trying hard to learn some dances.
With each twist, it trips and falls,
As laughter echoes through the walls.

A group of owls share tired jokes,
While beneath them, a squirrel strokes.
Its tail on the ground, a makeshift mic,
Let's hope it doesn't get too much hype!

## Symphonies of the Swaying Branches

Branches wave in the afternoon,
Calling out to passing raccoons.
With leaves as shakers, they have a blast,
Dancing to rhythms that never last.

A parrot squawks, adding his flair,
While pigeons join in without a care.
The whole grove sings, a silly tune,
Joining in joy, morning to noon!

## Memories in the Breeze

The wind whistles jokes from tree to tree,
Tickling leaves with such glee.
A branch sways and flicks a bee,
Who buzzes back, "Hey, watch with me!"

Caterpillars conga in a line,
Munching on leaves, feeling just fine.
But one brought lettuce, oh what a fuss,
"Not that, you silly, join in with us!"

## Hush of the Gentle Giants

In the woods where whispers play,
Leaves gossip like friends at noon.
Tall trunks sway with a silly sway,
 Underneath a bright blue moon.

Branches shrug with a cheeky grin,
 Squirrels dance, their tails a swirl.
 Birds dive and twirl, a bright din,
Nature's quirks make tempers whirl.

### Revelries in the Green Heart

Frogs croak tunes in a silly band,
Crickets join with a wink and nod.
Mice throw parties on the sand,
All is jolly in the oddest pod.

Twigs snap like laughter caught on air,
Leaves rustle secrets, shared delight.
Breeze tickles fur, a frolic there,
Nature's giggles, oh, what a sight!

**Parables of the Branches' Embrace**

Branches weave tales of curious fate,
Where owls hoot jokes in the night.
Raccoons debate while they allate,
Chasing shadows, a comical sight.

A slow sloth dangles, takes a rest,
Snoring louder than a rolling truck.
Life's just a game, it's all a jest,
Nature's humor can bring good luck.

## Memories in the Mist

Mists wrap around with a playful tease,
Hiding secrets of plant and tree.
Laughter dances in an evening breeze,
Whispers float where no one can see.

Picnics crash as winds play pranks,
Sandwiches fly like fickle kites.
Smiles erupt in the leafy flanks,
Nature's banter fills up the nights.

## Cadences in the Calm

In the shade where the branches sway,
A squirrel plans his acrobatics for the day.
He slips and trips on a sunlit beam,
Chasing shadows, lost in a dream.

A crow caws loud, thinks he's a star,
While a lizard sunbathes; the oddest bazaar.
They chirp and squabble in silly tone,
A symphony of chaos, nature's own.

## The Embrace of the Silent Grove

Beneath tall trunks, the breeze starts to dance,
A raccoon does a jig, seizing his chance.
He twirls and spins, with ungraceful flair,
As nearby, a turtle just doesn't care.

The ants hold a meeting, all dressed to impress,
While a snail's on a quest, but it's anyone's guess.
Funny how time moves at nature's sweet pace,
When life's just a race, at its own silly pace.

## **Breathless Moments in the Undergrowth**

Through tangled vines, a rabbit hops high,
Stumbling upon a butterfly flitting by.
With wiggly ears, he gives it a chase,
Only to trip, what a comical face!

A hedgehog rolls round in his prickly attire,
Falling flat on his back, he won't soon retire.
With giggles from parrots up high in the tree,
The whimsy of nature invites all to see.

## Carvings of Time in Wood and Stone

Old rocks whisper tales of the silliest past,
As a wise old owl gives a hoot that's a blast.
The squirrels tell stories, in hushed, jovial tones,
About acorns that rolled and made far-off moans.

A woodpecker knocks, a band on the rise,
While a cheeky raccoon plots his next surprise.
Nature's own laughter, a comic delight,
In the heart of the grove, where time takes its flight.

## The Silent Symphony of Nature

A bird on a branch sings out loud,
An awkward tune that makes us proud.
The rustling leaves join in the jest,
Nature's chorus at its best.

A squirrel darts, steals my sock,
While I sit here and try to talk.
His antics make me laugh and grin,
In this wild symphony, we all win.

The crickets chirp a silly beat,
While ants march on with tiny feet.
Each sound a splash of comic art,
In nature's show, we all take part.

So let's applaud this crazy sound,
Where laughter grows and joy is found.
In this silent symphony we sway,
Nature's fun is here to stay.

## Beneath the Emerald Veil

Under trees that seem to laugh,
A hidden path, a photograph.
With every step, a tale unfolds,
Of mischief, mayhem, and pure gold.

The shadows dance, the branches sway,
As quirky critters play away.
A rabbit hops, it trips, it flies,
With floppy ears and funny eyes.

The leaves gossip like school kids,
Whispering secrets, hiding bids.
While sunlight peeks through the green,
Caught in antics, quite the scene.

So under this veil, we find delight,
In nature's jest, our hearts take flight.
A moment shared in laughter's glow,
Beneath the emerald, life's a show.

## A Journey Through Leafy Whispers

Through leafy paths, we stroll along,
Where nature's humor feels so strong.
A bushy tail, a cackling crow,
Remind us all to take it slow.

The wind plays pranks, it pulls my hat,
While nearby, a fuzzy caterpillar chats.
With wiggly moves and playful grace,
It seems to put a smile on every face.

Each rustle wrapped in silly glee,
As flowers giggle, just wait and see.
A ladybug winks at me, too,
It knows the secrets of this view.

In leafy whispers, laughter thrives,
Nature's charm keeps us alive.
So join the fun, let your heart soar,
In this journey, we'll always want more.

## The Meeting of Tree and Sky

The trees reached up, with arms so wide,
While clouds look down with fluffy pride.
"Hello!" they shout, without a care,
As birds fly by to join the fair.

A branch is tickled by a breeze,
A squirrel hops to bridge the tease.
The sunbeam giggles, "Let's all play!"
In this conference, fun's on display.

With laughter shared, the leaves take flight,
Like confetti in a joy-filled sight.
The branches sway in rhythmic cheer,
As the sky laughs, "What are you doing here?"

At day's end, as twilight begins,
The giggling trees share whispered sins.
In this meeting, oh what a tie,
When tree and sky adore and fly.

## **Embers of Earth's Memory**

In the land where trees dance round,
Silly whispers in the breeze are found.
Leaves chuckle at the passerby's plight,
Trying to catch them in midday light.

Lizards wear sunglasses, quite the sight,
As they soak up sunshine, feeling so bright.
The ants are marching in a funky line,
Comparing their snacks, they're feeling fine.

Branches sway to a rhythm so bold,
Telling secrets of adventures long told.
With each rustle, there's mischief in play,
As squirrels plot their next nutty display.

Beneath those limbs, shadows play tricks,
Creating a stage for forest antics.
The groundhog pops up, gives a cheerful grin,
Caught in a game, where does he begin?

## The Tides of Leafy Henchmen

In a grove where leaves are firm allies,
Branches wave like mini samurai ties.
Laughing at winds that toss them around,
Swaying as if they're a comedy sound.

Saplings play soccer, with acorns galore,
Trying to score with a cheer and a roar.
The clumsy stumps trip, hilarious falls,
As laughter erupts from the grand old walls.

Raindrops drop in a free-fall race,
As puddles form mirrors, reflecting the face.
A crow caws jokes that get the sun's warm nod,
While nature bursts forth with giggles of God.

The fruit trees gossip, trading wild tales,
As butterflies dance, leaving vibrant trails.
In this world, nothing is quiet or meek,
It's a funny parade, every day of the week!

# Fragrance of Forgotten Dreams

The scent of laughter wafts through the air,
As daisies chuckle without a care.
Bumblebees buzz with old rhymes to share,
While dandelions play hairstylist with flair.

Old stones recline, telling stories of yore,
As mushrooms throw parties, rich with folklore.
A rabbit hops in, with socks mismatched,
Claiming it's fashion, with tails attached.

Sunflowers wave in a ridiculous dance,
Joking about bees who take every chance.
Petals flicker, a carnival show,
As they bask in the sun, stealing the glow.

Night falls softly, the moon cracks a smile,
While crickets chirp tunes that stretch for a mile.
In dreams, they spill tales of giggles and cheer,
Embodying joy that lingers so near.

## The Harmonics of Nature's Breath

The wind hums softly, in quirky delight,
Playing a tune, like a witty sprite.
Leaves clap together, a comedic round,
While the trees giggle at sounds they have found.

Frogs croak symphonies, offbeat and bold,
While fireflies wiggle, like stories retold.
Each flash is a punchline, sparkling bright,
As critters join in, crafting laughter all night.

Chirps and yips mix in a joyful refrain,
While the stars giggle down, feeling no pain.
A hedgehog rolls by, in a tuxedo of leaves,
Bowing to the crowd, as everyone believes.

Nature's orchestra plays with whimsical flair,
Every riff and giggle, like a breath of fresh air.
Where paws meet the ground, and wings take a trot,
It's a medley of whimsy, right on the spot!

## The Realm of Leafy Dreams

In a forest of quirks, the trees wear a grin,
Their branches like arms waving, let the fun begin!
Squirrels throw parties, with acorns as treats,
Dancing on roots with the funniest feats.

Beneath the bright moon, the koalas align,
They practice their stand-up, delivering punchlines.
With puns on the leaves and jokes in the breeze,
Laughter erupts, putting worries at ease.

A platypus sings, with a voice like a croak,
His friends are all giggling, it's all just a joke.
With feathery friends, they join for the show,
Making merry the night, letting chuckles just flow.

In the realm of the leafy, the laughter is bright,
As shadows join in for a whimsical sight.
With every soft rustle, new giggles are found,
In the land of the green, where joy does abound.

## Hidden Messages Among the Roots

In a tangle of greenery, secrets are shared,
With whispers of wisdom, the trees have declared.
Their gnarled old branches spread rumors so wild,
While the grass giggles softly, like a playful child.

Beneath the bold trunks, the carrots conspire,
With radishes scheming, their plans never tire.
They chuckle at humans who simply walk by,
Oblivious to antics that stir in the sky.

A duck wobbles over, quacking in rhyme,
As he flaps through the flowers, having the best time.
The lilies start laughing, their petals a-flutter,
With jokes about worms, and a dance in the butter.

Down in the depths, where the roots intertwine,
The gossip of earthworms is surely divine.
With humorous tales of the world up above,
Nature's own jesters, surrounded by love.

## **Echoing Dreams of the Green**

In the forest a parrot jokes,
Singing tunes, while the woodpecker pokes.
A koala swings, trying to dance,
But his moves are more like a trance.

The leaves giggle, rustling in glee,
As a pine tree tries to play tag with a bee.
A dingo bursts out in a fiery chase,
Trips on roots, oh, what a face!

Wombats watch, chuckling in shade,
As lizards play leapfrog, unafraid.
Ants march along like a tiny parade,
While the sun laughs with a warm cascade.

In this realm where laughter reigns,
Nature's whimsy spills through the lanes.
Each breath, a chuckle, each moment a tease,
In this green world, we find our ease.

## Imagery in the Wilderness

A wallaby with a quirky grin,
Wearing a hat, where shall we begin?
He hops in rhythm, a dance so fine,
With a bushy-tailed friend, sipping wine.

The trees sway, making jokes in the breeze,
Swaying left and right, like playful tease.
A creature chortles from up in a branch,
While the flowers wiggle, begging a chance.

A snake in shades, with tales to share,
Slides down the trunk, unaware of the dare.
As a hedgehog sings, crooning in tune,
The moon chuckles softly, beneath the rune.

The wilderness buzzes, a circus alive,
With laughter and antics, it seems to thrive.
Amidst all the fun, sanity's lost,
In this wild world, joy's the only cost.

## The Tranquil Chorus of Woodlands

In the stillness, a frog begins to croak,
Each note a giggle, a playful poke.
The crickets join in, a symphony bright,
As fireflies twinkle, igniting the night.

But watch out! A turtle, slow as could be,
Stumbles upon a cat, who yells, "Not me!"
They chase through the ferns, a funny ballet,
With squirrel spectators, they cheer all the way.

A bluejay swoops down, mockingly calls,
While chipmunks play tag, bouncing off walls.
Nature's notebook filled with these quirks,
Each page turns, revealing more smirks.

In this chorus of whimsy, life's never bland,
Every twig whispers secrets, oh, isn't it grand?
Between laughter and chirps, joy weaves a thread,
In the woodland's embrace, all worries are shed.

## Secrets of the Flora

Beneath the blossoms, secrets abound,
Mice in bow ties gather around.
A daisy winks, sharing a plot,
While a butterfly chuckles, looking quite hot.

The sunflowers gossip, plotting a scheme,
While the clover chuckles at a whimsical dream.
And amidst it all, a cactus with style,
Holds a dance-off, brings everyone a smile.

A rose tries to rhyme, but thorns get in way,
As daisies roll laughter, brightening the day.
The ferns sway to humor, like gentle waves,
In the garden of wonders, all mischief behaves.

With petals and laughter, a festival grows,
Nature's tales blend, like the wind that blows.
In this funny patch where colors explode,
The secrets of flora brighten the road.

## Harmonies of the Dappled Light

In the grove where shadows play,
Squirrels dance by light of day.
They wear hats, quite out of style,
On tiny heads, they strut in style.

A bird sings off-key, oh what a sight,
It tries to charm, but gets things wrong,
The notes stagger like a drunk on the flight,
Yet still, the sun shines, all day long.

A rabbit hops, with shoes too big,
It trips and tumbles, does a jig.
Chasing shadows, chasing dreams,
Elusive laughter in sunbeams.

So when the leaves, they start to sway,
Join in the fun and dance today.
Life is silly, wild, and bright,
In the grove, all feels just right.

## **Breath of the Soft Earth**


Down by the creek, the frogs have a chat,
With lilypads on their heads, looking quite fat.
They croak out jokes that miss the mark,
Ribbiting laughter from dawn till dark.

A turtle strolls with a swagger so bold,
His shell is a kitchen, he's cooking up gold.
With a pinch of sass and a dash of cheer,
He claims he's the chef of the year!

Among the flowers, a bee starts to hum,
Buzzing about like a little drum.
It slips on a petal, what a big blunder,
And lands in a cupcake, isn't that thunder?

As night approaches, the crickets unite,
Their concert begins, oh what a fright!
The claps that echo, a comedic scene,
Nature's orchestra, a silly routine.

# Layers of Memory in the Glade

Within this glade, the stories unfold,
Of a hedgehog who wears socks, so bold.
He claims they're lucky, brings good cheer,
Though they smell like old cheese—oh dear!

Old trees gossip, with knots and grooves,
One pulls a face, another just moves.
They talk about squirrels, their acorn stash,
And the neighbor's cat who makes a splash!

A fox wearing glasses, a scholar he swears,
Reads books on plants with delicate airs.
He squints at the pages, then gets quite vexed,
Turns out he's read them all out of context!

So here in the glade of tales we see,
Nature's own comedy spree.
From funny critters to trees that snooze,
Each layer reveals a world we can't lose.

## Tranquil Whispers at Twilight

As the sun dips low, the crickets conspire,
Under the stars, the night feels like fire.
A raccoon in pajamas, so snug and tight,
Tries to steal cookies, what a delight!

The owls hoot riddles, all wise and sly,
With head tilts that make you wonder why.
They misplace their wisdom, it seems, in jest,
"Whooo's the coolest?" they chant, quite impressed.

A moth dances round like it's on a spree,
Dazzled by lights that will never flee.
It twirls and it spins, what a strange sight,
In love with a bulb, what a silly night.

So linger awhile as the stars start to gleam,
With laughter and giggles, let's join in the dream.
Under the night sky, let merriment spread,
With shadows and sillies, let joy be our thread.

## Reflections in the Lush Green

In the garden, frogs hold court,
Telling tales of their brave sport.
With a splash and a leap so grand,
They embarrass the worms on land.

Kangaroos in a hop-along race,
Chasing shadows across the place.
All while a platypus sneers,
At land creatures and all their fears.

The sun sets, and laughter blends,
As critters gather, new fun extends.
With tea made of dew, giggles arise,
Over bugs that dance in bright, silly skies.

As night falls, the laughter unfolds,
A chorus of beasts with stories bold.
In the lush greenery, spirits take flight,
Where nature's antics bring pure delight.

## **Rustling Tales of the Wild**

Squirrels plot in their secret huddle,
Stealing acorns, oh what a muddle!
A bird squawks, clashing their plans,
As they wiggle away with full hands.

Down by the stream, a beaver grins,
While fish tease with their slippery fins.
"Catch me!" they bubble, with splashes so bold,
While turtles roll, all snug in their hold.

Lizards sunbathe, bragging with flair,
Boasting tales of who's toughest out there.
While ants march by, quite the parade,
"Follow us, or forever be swayed!"

At dusk, the laughter fills the air,
With friendships found in fun debonair.
Every day a new story begins,
In the wild where they giggle and grin.

## Secrets Carried by the Wind

The breeze whispers secrets, oh so sly,
As leaves wiggle and flutter up high.
A gust sends the seeds on their way,
To places where silly games play.

Bees buzz loudly, shaking their heads,
Complaining of flowers sharing their beds.
"Move over!" they hum, with such attitude,
While the petals blush in their bright mood.

A kite gets tangled, caught in a tree,
The kids all squeal, 'Oh woe is he!'
But with laughter they free him, high in the sky,
Not a care as they wave goodbye.

Under the moon's grin, tales persist,
As nature joins in, none want to miss.
With every gust, new laughter spins,
Through the whispers of joy where fun begins.

## Dance of the Forgotten Leaves

Leaves twirl down in a playful waltz,
Whispering tales of nature's antics, not faults.
A pinecone sighs with a plop to the ground,
While crickets join in with chirps all around.

A turtle napping under a big shade,
Awakens to laughter, his peaceful charade.
"Oh dear!" he shouts, as he wobbles and rolls,
"It's hard being slow in this world of bold souls!"

A raccoon in shadows strikes a grand pose,
"I'm the king of the night!" he proudly bestows.
His crown made of twigs sends giggles galore,
As the moonlight encourages even more.

With each twinkling star, the night comes alive,
As critters unite, in fun they thrive.
In nature's dance, all find their groove,
A merry occasion where no one can lose.

**Stories in the Shade**

Beneath the trees, we laugh and play,
With squirrels scheming all the day.
A branch just shook, what could it be?
A bird or just a sneezy bee?

The shadows dance, they twist and twirl,
While leafy hats begin to swirl.
We build our forts with sticks and twine,
And crown ourselves with leaves divine.

Laying back, we spot the sky,
Why's that cloud shaped like a pie?
We train to catch the falling nuts,
But end up dodging sneaky huts.

In summer's warmth, we find delight,
While ants hold a parade at night.
With giggles, we shall rule this glade,
And share the tales that never fade.

## Cadence of the Timbered Path


On paths where giggles bounce and roam,
We skip and jump, it feels like home.
The bark may scratch, but we won't mind,
We'll name that tree, 'The Great Big Kind.'

With each step, the leaves like confetti,
A dance of nature, oh-so-settle.
We pause to see a lizard strut,
Deciding if he's bold or just a nut.

Rooty carpets make us trip,
But laughter saves us from the slip.
We race the breeze, we voice our calls,
As echoes bounce from towering walls.

In every twist, the stories grow,
With friends beside, we steal the show.
So let us wander without a map,
In laughter's arms, we take a nap.

## Calls from the Leafy Canopy

Above us, chatter fills the air,
A parrot's joke, a monkey's dare.
"Who stole my fruit?" cries one in green,
A fruity tussle, quite the scene!

With leaves that rustle, secrets spill,
A choir of critters, what a thrill!
The sun peeks in, a playful tease,
While shadows dance with utmost ease.

The acorns roll like bowling balls,
As nutty thoughts replace the calls.
We laugh at all the wobbly sights,
Without a care for silly heights.

Among the branches, joy takes flight,
With jokes that linger, day to night.
The canopy's a stage so grand,
With nature's antics, oh so planned.

## The Echo of Nature's Breath

In a forest full of whimsy bright,
The trees hold lessons, pure delight.
They chuckle low with every breeze,
As leaves spill whispers with such ease.

We march along on mossy ground,
Our laughter bounces all around.
A bumblebee with a wiggly dance,
Invites us all to join the prance.

With ghosts of giggles in the glen,
We find the gnomes are here again.
They pitch their tents, all smiles and cheer,
Their jokes are tall, we can't get near!

As dusk enfolds, the trails come alive,
Frogs croak stories that surely thrive.
In nature's rhythm, we find our peace,
A symphony of fun will never cease.

# Reverent Calls from the Canopy

When the leaves start to whisper, they giggle and tease,
The branches shake wildly, swaying with ease.
The squirrels of mischief, they leap and they bound,
With nutty ambitions, they dance all around.

A parrot's wise chatter, a joke in the breeze,
A flock full of laughter puts everyone at ease.
"Why did the tree cross the road?" they all caw,
"To show off its bark, and to just be a saw!"

A gentle wind carries a rumor or two,
Of koalas in pajamas, sipping on dew.
They snooze on the high limbs, checking their phones,
With dreams of eucalyptus-flavored ice cones.

Sun-glinted leaves shimmy with each passing joke,
As nature's comedians share quips with a poke.
In this laughter-filled haven, where humor runs free,
The canopy chuckles, just wait and you'll see.

## The Language of Sunlit Glades

In the glade where the sunlight just loves to play,
Trees whisper sweet nothings, in their own goofy way.
"Did you hear about pine, who sang with a lilt?
His voice was so smooth, we thought he was built!"

A cheeky breeze giggles, wrapping around trunks,
Tickling all leaves, in their green, leafy spunks.
"Why don't you see us when we're up in the sky?
We're experts at jokes, but a sight that's so shy!"

And the daisies, they chime in, "We're blooming with glee!
With petals like confetti, we're the party, you see!"
As shadows dance lightly, bugs join in the fun,
A rollicking rollick, till the day's nearly done.

In the sweet sunlit glades, where laughter is grown,
The humor of nature, by all seeds is sown.
So step lightly along, and share in a cheer,
For life in the sunlight is simply sincere.

## The Scent of Verdant Remembrance

The leaves dance and sway with grace,
As squirrels trickster race in place.
A breeze carries laughter, oh so bright,
In this green realm, a pure delight.

The branches whisper jokes at night,
As owls hoot in sheer delight.
The trees chuckle with each tiny breeze,
Their humor tickles, puts minds at ease.

The sun peeks through like a shy friend,
Each shadow a reminder, around the bend.
A bark that barks, how odd it seems,
In this wild world where nothing's as it seems.

With every rustle, a tale unfolds,
Of cheeky critters, adventures bold.
Oh how nature loves to play,
In this green haven every day.

## **Silhouettes of Serene Mornings**

In morning light, the trees do tease,
Their branches twist, they shimmy with ease.
A gentle sway, a giggle or two,
As morning mist paints the world anew.

Chirping friends sing a funny tune,
While blossoms dance beneath the moon.
Dewdrops giggle, upon a leaf,
Nature's comedy, a bright relief.

The sun peers in, a golden grin,
While Kookaburras laugh from within.
They chatter on about the day's plan,
Crafting mischief, more fun than a man.

With twitching leaves and playful sway,
Serene mornings bring the funniest play.
In this leafy realm, all worries cease,
As we share a smile, nature's peace.

## Songs of the Bark and Blossom

Beneath the boughs, where shadows swing,
The little critters dance and sing.
Bark that talks and blossoms that giggle,
In a world where mischief makes us wiggle.

A parrot with tales that twist and shout,
Says the squirrel can't gather, he's just about.
A fig that fell with a plop and a pop,
Turning nature into a comedic hop.

Their antics in the sun make us grin,
While the trees watch on with a wise spin.
Frogs in the pond join the playful show,
Croaking to the rhythm, go with the flow.

As petals tumble like laughter in air,
There's joy and wit everywhere.
A leaf, a bark, a blossom's jest,
In nature's folly, we find our rest.

## Beneath the Boughs of Time

Underneath the grand old tree,
Wise branches whisper foolishly.
Time giggles as the leaves exchange,
Secrets of life, a bit deranged.

The sunbeams prance with a silly flare,
While critters plot without a care.
A game of hide and seek, how fun!
In this world, we all can run.

The roots tap dance on fertile ground,
With stories that echo all around.
A fruit that rolls, a nut that slips,
Nature's comedy takes funny trips.

So take a seat, relax a while,
Let nature's humor bring a smile.
For under these boughs, both thick and fine,
Every moment dances, divine.

## Whispers Among the Leaves

The leaves are giggling high,
As birds wear laughter as a tie.
Squirrels dance on branches bold,
Making jokes we've never told.

The rustling sounds a secret jest,
While wind pulls pranks, it's quite the fest.
A koala snores a comical tune,
Dreaming of dancin' under the moon.

Laughter bounces off the bark,
As shadows play a funny lark.
Down below, a rabbit hops,
Spilling tea, and then he stops.

With nature's joke, we join the spree,
In this leafy comedy, wild and free.

## **Resonance of the Green Canopy**

Up above, the leaves all scheme,
Plotting pranks, a leafy dream.
The cicadas play the drums,
While lizards wear their little plums.

Branches sway with giggling glee,
As mossy slippers dance with spree.
Beneath the shade, a lizard grins,
His buddy sneezes; chaos begins.

Silly shadows throw a ball,
Each branch becomes a lively hall.
The canopy has tales to share,
Of cheeky squirrels and funny hair.

In this green world, we all chuckle,
As nature hides its playful chuckle.

## Shadows Beneath the Tall Trees

In the shade, whispers politely roar,
As ants march off to the bistro's door.
Trees gossip through their waving limbs,
While sunbeams dance to nature's whims.

Beneath the trunks, a frog takes a seat,
With a crown made from leftover beet.
A gum tree shares its sticky stories,
Of raccoons' late-night glories.

A breeze tickles all who dare,
Leaves crack jokes that float in air.
Under the boughs, giggles swell,
As birds hold court, oh what a spell!

So gather round to hear this fun,
Where shadows play, and laughs weigh a ton.

**Songs of the Silvery Bark**

The bark sings softly, a tune so bright,
While critters join in with all their might.
A koala strums a leaf guitar,
Singing ballads from near and far.

Near the roots, a chipmunk sways,
Making up lyrics to sunny days.
With each note, the foliage shakes,
Fluttering wings and laughter wakes.

Branches sway, keeping time with glee,
As bees buzz along, in harmony.
The jokes within the rustling sound,
Leave all who hear, delightfully bound.

So let's celebrate this leafy show,
With songs that tickle down below.

## A Symphony of Rustling Foliage

In the breeze, the leaves do dance,
Whispering secrets, taking a chance.
A koala's snore, a parrot's cheer,
Nature's symphony, loud and clear.

Swaying branches, a comical sight,
A squirrel slips, gives humans a fright.
Raccoon antics under the moon,
While crickets hum a tuneful tune.

A cicada's song, a frog's delight,
Bugs in chorus, what a strange sight!
The rustling trees, like friends at play,
In their green jackets, bright and gay.

Oh, what fun in this leafy place,
With each twist and turn, a new face.
The orchestra of the wild and free,
Turns nature's stage to a comedy.

## The Language of the Air

The wind carries tales, a cheeky breeze,
Tickling the leaves with the greatest of ease.
A dingo howls, thinking he's grand,
While lizards lounge, toes in the sand.

"Who's up there?" asks a nosy crow,
As branches sway, moving to and fro.
The sky holds laughter, the clouds just tease,
While cactus cats dance, aiming to please.

The whispers of insects, a quirky throng,
Chatting away like they all belong.
The sun sets low, shadows waving 'hi',
While bats audition for a night-time sky.

Laughter lingers in this leafy space,
Nature's sense of humor, a shared embrace.
In the language of air, we find our tune,
With giggles and sighs, from morn till noon.

## **Veils of Mist in the Twilit Forest**

As mist rolls in, things take a twist,
Where shadows lurk, and ducks coexist.
Bats in tuxedos, all set to fly,
And owls giggle, 'Cause who can deny?

A fox in a scarf, on a midnight stroll,
Tripping on roots, losing control.
The branches chuckle, the stones throw shade,
While fireflies plan a parade, unafraid.

Fog wraps the trees, a cozy embrace,
Where every creature finds their place.
The tales of the forest, a slapstick show,
Replays and rewrites, as the winds blow.

In this dreamy gloom, odd friends collide,
With chuckles and quirks, there's nowhere to hide.
Every nook and cranny, a giggle just right,
As the veil of mist winks at the night.

## Stories Woven Through the Canopy

Woven with laughter, the branches spread,
Quirky creatures pop up to say, 'Hello, Fred!'
A wallaby hops, sporting a hat,
While a lizard chuckles, "Well, imagine that!"

The sun's rays peek through the leafy weave,
Highlighting a tale that you won't believe.
A party of parrots, with dance moves outrageous,
Making the day feel rather contagious.

A sloth takes a selfie, oh what a sight,
As mushrooms gaze up, their faces alight.
The canopy sways with stories galore,
Of mischief and laughter, forevermore.

Each branch a chapter, with humor and flair,
The forest giggles, with tales to share.
Stories woven in this leafy land,
With laughter and joy, forever hand in hand.

## Dreaming Under the Sprawling Canopy

Swaying trees whisper tales of light,
A koala's snore in our dream-filled night.
Beneath the leaves, we dance and twirl,
While squirrels plot out their acorn whirl.

The branches stretch like a giant's hand,
Pinecone missiles in a playful band.
Laughter rings as the shadows play,
In this delightful, leafy ballet.

## Melodies of the Fertile Ground

A symphony of crickets starts to sing,
As worms tune up for a grand spring fling.
Dancing ants march to their own sweet beat,
While snails are slow in their sticky retreat.

The soil hums with laughter and delight,
As roots high-five in the soft moonlight.
Every critter joins in the joyful fun,
Making music till the night is done.

## **Reflections of a Verdant World**

In the pond, frogs wear crowns of mud,
As lily pads float like boats in a flood.
Dragonflies zoom in a hurried race,
While turtles lounge with a leisurely grace.

Beneath the sun, plant talks are absurd,
"How's it growing?" asks a friendly bird.
Every leaf knows how to crack a joke,
In a laughter-filled, greeny cloak.

## **Breath of Summer's Shade**

Breezes play tag with the grass below,
As we snooze in the shade, moving slow.
A friend's wild hat flies up like a kite,
While bees buzz past as they take their flight.

The sun's warm smile brings a gentle tease,
And ants hold hands in a wobbly squeeze.
With snacks of fruit, we giggle and munch,
In this silly, sun-kissed picnic crunch.

## Flight of the Evening Zephyr

The breeze that tickles, just a tease,
Through leaves it dances, with playful ease.
It whispers secrets, then takes flight,
A game of tag, from day to night.

The branches sway, in wild delight,
While insects laugh and take their bite.
They waltz in pairs, no care in sight,
Oh, what a show! It's quite the sight!

The shadows twist, they hop and roam,
In this green maze, we feel at home.
A squirrel pops up, with cheeky grin,
Then scurries off, oh where's he been?

So hear the laughter, feel the cheer,
Nature's comedy, so vivid here.
In every rustle, giggles bloom,
The forest's joke, it lifts the gloom.

## Colors of a Forgotten Dream

A splash of green, a dash of brown,
The leaves wear crowns of nature's gown.
In sunlight's glow, they wink and sway,
Reminding us to laugh all day.

A bluebird fluffs, it strikes a pose,
With feathers bright, like a circus rose.
It cocked its head, then gave a cheer,
As if to say, 'Hey, life is here!'

A moth with shades of golden hue,
Tries to impress a flower too.
She flips and flutters with such flair,
"Oh, what a sight! Come see! I swear!"

In this wild art, no rules apply,
Just joyful whims beneath the sky.
Colors dance, they spin and gleam,
In laughter's light, we chase the dream.

## Whispers in the Canopy

High above, the leaves conspire,
With giggles soft, that never tire.
They gossip low, about the breeze,
"And did you hear? Just come and see!"

A branch holds court, the acorns plead,
"We're wiser now, we are the seed!"
They share their tales with grand delight,
"Remember last week? What a fright!"

A squirrel chimes in with a jest,
"Life's a game, and I'm the best!"
He twirls and spins, a little clown,
Then scampers off, but won't back down.

So listen close, to nature's friends,
Their laughter echoes, never ends.
In this green realm, it's all a play,
Where joy takes flight and leads the way.

## Beneath the Silver Leaves

Beneath the silver, shadows stretch,
Where funny tales the branches fetch.
A lizard struts, with stylish flair,
He tips his hat, as if to share.

A crow caws loud, like he's on stage,
"Just watch me now! I'm full of rage!"
But soon he laughs, and flips his wing,
In this great show, he's the king.

A rabbit hops with bouncy glee,
"A magic trick? Come watch me, see!"
He disappears behind a shrub,
Returning fast, with quite the grub!

So gather 'round, let laughter sway,
In this grand play, we find the way.
Among the green, the tales we weave,
With funny friends, we choose to believe.

## Serenity in the Gentle Scent

The leaves they chatter, whisper sweet,
As squirrels practice their acorn beat.
A kangaroo jumps, but oh, what a fall!
Even the parakeets take a guffaw.

The gum trees sway, in a silly dance,
While bees are buzzing, lost in a trance.
A koala yawns, and drops from the height,
In the land of giggles, everything's light.

With laughter ringing through branches tall,
The lizards skitter, their shadows small.
A wombat sighs, but can't sleep a wink,
As the whole forest sways, what do you think?

So breathe in deep, the joy even more,
In this backdrop of fun, who could ignore?
The breeze gives a nudge, wind's playful game,
Nature is laughing, it's never the same.

## Chants of the Meadow Mist

In the misty morn, a rabbit does jig,
He hops through the grass, oh, just look at him dig.
While ducks tell tales of their nightly dreams,
The geese join in with their silly screams.

Forget not the chickens, all dressed in cluck,
They strut with the pride of a fancy truck.
Caterpillars wiggle, their costumes so bright,
Reminding us all, that wrong can feel right.

A breeze carrying giggles from hill to hill,
The flowers all chuckle, it's quite the thrill.
The daisies wink, as the sun starts to rise,
In this meadow of fun, we cannot disguise.

So dance with the shadows, and laugh with the sun,
In this chorus of joy, all hearts weigh a ton.
For in silly moments, life finds its tune,
As we're singing along with the birds and the moon.

# Timeless Tales in the Stillness

In a sleepy grove, where stories unwind,
An owl tells jokes, of the woodland kind.
A turtle cracks up, slow in his ways,
While a chipmunk snickers, with cheeks in a craze.

The breeze whispers gossips, oh what a yarn,
Of raccoons stealing snacks from the barn.
A fox rolls over, plays dead on the spot,
But giggles from all just can't be forgot.

Trees commentate the events of the hour,
While ferns flutter softly, with supernatural power.
A hedgehog's remark brings a hearty swoon,
Lively debates under the bright afternoon.

In this woodland theatre, the fun is so grand,
Each laugh is a note, in nature's own band.
So grab a seat, come join the spree,
As stories unfold, wild, happy, and free.

# Fables of the Winding Roots

As roots twist and tangle underfoot,
A wise old snail puts on his best suit.
He tells grand tales of the dirt and the rain,
Each drop a laugh, a sprinkle of sane.

The fungi giggle in colors so bright,
When shadows play tag in the soft twilight.
A family of ants put on a parade,
With crumbs as their trophies, they simply invade.

Underneath the moss, a party begins,
As fireflies ignite, like shiny pins.
The crickets sing, with a rhythmic refrain,
Turning the night into a whimsical gain.

So let the roots whisper, share all their lore,
Of laughter and joy found in each hidden door.
In this quirky world where the wild things roam,
Every twist and turn leads the heart to its home.

## **Nature's Harmonious Lullaby**

In the woods, a frog starts to sing,
A chorus of bugs joins in on the fling.
The birds are all laughing, the squirrels on a spree,
As a bear tries to dance, just look at him flee!

The breeze has a wiggle, the flowers a grin,
While the trees chuckle softly, like they're all kin.
A rabbit hops giggling, a fox tries to rhyme,
In this symphony silly, all nature's in time.

The sun's peeking down, like a kid on a swing,
While bees buzz around, like they just won a fling.
Each rustle and rustle brings laughter anew,
As nature conspires with antics to view.

So join in the fun, bring your song and your cheer,
With whimsy and joy around every sphere.
From the roots to the sky, let the laughter resound,
In the sweetest of melodies that nature has found.

## The Spirit of the Evergreen

In a forest so green, where the pine trees tease,
The squirrels hold court, munching nuts with ease.
They jest and they jive in their own little way,
While the owls roll their eyes, like, 'Not another play!'

The pine needles giggle, they tickle the ground,
With every soft step, a soft whispering sound.
The rabbits play hopscotch, the badgers all cheer,
While the deers take a bow, as they pass with a leer.

A breeze blows through branches, like gossip in town,
As the trees sway and chuckle, the leaves twirl around.
The sun winks playfully, so bright in the sky,
Even thunder gets jealous, but it's not shy!

With nature's comedians, there's laughter to share,
In a world full of joy, free of worry and care.
Come dance with the critters, join in on the fun,
For the spirit of green never shuns anyone!

## **Lullabies Among the Leaves**

In the canopy high, where the laughter resides,
The leaves sing soft tunes, like merry little guides.
A brood of bright sparrows chime in for the show,
While the ants form a band, stealing seeds from below.

A snail takes a stroll, slow as syrupy breeze,
While the ladybugs giggle, floating high with ease.
The shadows are playful, drawing shapes on the ground,
In this leafy amphitheater where chuckles abound.

The softest of whispers slips through every tree,
As the dandelions dance, wild and carefree.
The worms do the worm, on the soft blanket earth,
Celebrating this nature's most humorous birth.

So gather your friends, there's a party tonight,
With the stars as our guests and the moon shining bright.
In the lull of the leaves, find your joy so divine,
In a world that's all funny, where the stars intertwine.

# The Dance of the Whispering Branches

Oh, the trees are all swaying, like dance partners bold,
With the wind as their leader, a sight to behold.
A raccoon joins in, with his wild furry flair,
While the owls shake their feathers, 'It's quite debonair!'

The branches all whisper, telling secrets in tune,
While the sunbeams are nodding, they're over the moon.
The bunnies leap awkwardly, trying to conjoin,
But trip over roots, and that's how they join!

A badger does a twirl, oh what a delight,
As the crickets keep time, with their chirps through the night.
Each rustle a giggle, as leaves join the spree,
Creating a ruckus in the forest, so free.

With laughter and joy, the woodlands all sway,
As the branches keep dancing, come join in the play.
So grab your best pal, let's twirl and let's spin,
In the realm of the giggles, where the fun's just begun!

## Murmurs in the Sunlit Grove

In a grove where bright leaves sway,
Squirrels shout and shout hooray!
A bird takes flight, then hits a tree,
I laugh so hard, oh what a spree!

A lizard dons a straw hat bold,
Claims he's the king of sunlit gold!
He dances with a flower's sway,
Announcing spring is here to stay!

A butterfly with quite the flair,
Wobbles by without a care!
The breeze joins in, a ticklish tease,
As ants march on with firm decrees!

Beneath the sun, the joy runs free,
Nature's laughter is the key!
With every rustle, the fun expands,
In this grove where whimsy stands!

## Crescendo of the Forest Breeze

A gust whirls by with a cheeky grin,
Tickling leaves like they're kin!
A chipmunk tumbles, fluff in tow,
Yelling 'Catch me if you know!'

Branches sway, a comical dance,
Nature's stage, a bright romance!
Crisp laughter bounces, soft and bright,
Drawing giggles from day to night!

Giggling ferns and chuckling vines,
Join the spree with silly signs!
A young raccoon steals a snack,
Then scurries off without a track!

With every breeze, the forest glows,
It's a symphony, that's how it goes!
Amidst this glee, we can't refrain,
Just join the laughter, feel no pain!

## Beneath the Swaying Branches

Beneath the branches, shadows play,
Where a rabbit sings, 'What a day!'
A wise old owl hoots a tune,
While frogs croak out beneath the moon!

A dance-off starts between the bees,
They show their moves, oh so with ease!
Frolicsome roots try to jump,
Bumping their heads in a leafy thump!

As bugs exchange their crafted jokes,
A gopher sneezes, oh what hoax!
With giggles bursting all around,
Nature's laughter is profoundly found!

The breeze chuckles, it can't resist,
At all the shenanigans persist!
Beneath the sway, all moods align,
In this wild party, it's simply divine!

## Reflections in the Soft Moonlight

Under the moon's soft, silvery beam,
Rabbits gossip, or so it seems!
A raccoon juggles apples bright,
While owls hoot, 'What a sight!'

The river laughs, a bubbly tune,
Reflecting stars to welcome June!
Fireflies twirl, a dance on cue,
Winking at all, just me and you!

Crickets chirp their nightly song,
As shadows stretch, all night long!
A frog strikes a pose, a diva grand,
While flowers sway in a laughing band!

In this glow, where jesters play,
The world's a comedy come what may!
In the moonlight, let spirits soar,
As laughter rings forevermore!

## **Glimpses through the Leaves**

In the breeze, the branches sway,
Hiding secrets they won't relay.
Silly whispers, rustling tricks,
Leaves giggle, playing with sticks.

Sunbeams dance and twirl about,
Shadows leap and laugh, no doubt.
A squirrel chats with a lost crow,
Dueling with acorns in tow.

Bugs march in quirky lines,
Trading stories of grapevines.
Poky thorns join in the fun,
What a sight, it's never done!

Nature's party, oh what a sight,
In this leafy realm, pure delight.
Come join the laughter, take a peek,
At playful chaos, so unique.

## The Poetry of the Wind's Caress

The wind tickles many a leaf,
Tickling tales beyond belief.
A dance of petals, round and round,
Laughter lingers in the sound.

Caterpillars twirl in delight,
Spinning silk under moonlight.
A clumsy bird tries to sing,
But trips on air—oh, what a fling!

Around the branches chatter flows,
In an orchestra of snorts and woes.
Each gust, a punchline in the air,
Nature's humor, everywhere!

Clouds roll by with silly grins,
Laughing like children, playing in spins.
Here, mirth and greenery entwine,
Blowing sweet verses, oh how divine!

## Nature's Gentle Serenade

Hummingbirds zoom in a silly race,
Rounding trees at dizzying pace.
Whispers of grass beneath the sun,
A plush landscape where giggles run.

Frogs croak sonnets out of tune,
Mice bring harmony to the moon.
Each creature's laugh rings loud and clear,
In this concert where joy is near.

The daisies nod, sharing their jokes,
While tumbleweeds roll, playing folks.
With ferns in whiskers, smiles abound,
Nature's laughter knows no bound.

The brook babbles with a grin,
Nature's chuckle pulls you in.
Join the rhyme of joyous trees,
In this serenade, feel the breeze!

## Harmonies of the Hushed Woods

In the twilight, a chorus hums,
A symphony of snickers and drums.
Whimsical shadows play tag at night,
With giggles that sparkle, oh what a sight!

Mice wear hats made of tiny leaves,
While crafty owls weave tales with ease.
Under a willow, laughs have a ball,
Nature's comedy, here for all.

A raccoon juggles acorns with flair,
As fireflies giggle, lighting the air.
Crickets chirp, composing their songs,
In this madness, everything belongs.

With every rustle, joy takes flight,
In the hush of the woods, pure delight.
Join the revelry, dance with the night,
For laughter and nature dance side by side!

# Lament of the Old Trees

In the forest, the old trees sigh,
Barking jokes as the branches fly.
Their leaves chuckle with a raucous tone,
While squirrels giggle, never alone.

In twilight's dance, they've seen it all,
Acorns bouncing, oh what a ball!
With roots deep in stories they weave,
They laugh at the mischief we believe.

When the wind whispers secrets low,
They ponder the times of long, long ago.
Each flip of a leaf, a tale to share,
Of awkward birds and their clumsy flair.

Still standing there, with wisdom wide,
They wave at the critters that scurry and glide.
In every creak, a punchline awaits,
Old trees turning silly, despite their great states.

## The Breath of Nature's Spirit

The flowers bloom in a riotous spree,
Dancing around like they're bursting with glee.
Bees buzzing by with a silly hum,
Whirling in circles, oh what a drum!

The clouds giggle, shadowing the ground,
As raindrops, like laughter, fall all around.
Sunbeams burst forth in delightful delight,
Chasing the shadows with playful light!

Even the breeze, with its whooshing song,
Whispers of nature where all things belong.
In this grand symphony, humor does thrive,
As life takes the stage, feeling so alive!

With ants on parade and frogs' funky tunes,
Life's a carnival beneath the soft moons.
Every creature's a comic, every plant a clown,
In the kaleidoscope world where laughter's renown.

## Visions of Verdure and Light

In the greens where the sunlight plays,
Laughter leaps through the colorful bays.
Each leaf a jester, each stem a cheer,
In the festival of foliage, nothing's austere.

Beetles boogie on the bark so stout,
With nature's rhythm, they twist and shout.
While ferns flutter in their witty dress,
They throw a party, oh what a mess!

The daisies chime with giggling grace,
As they wave hello in a sunlit embrace.
Meanwhile, the grass throws a ticklish dance,
With mischievous wiggles, they prance and prance.

In every corner, a vibrant jest,
With nature's humor, we are so blessed.
The canopy chuckles, the landscape beams,
In this playful world, we collect our dreams.

## Tapestry of Twilight Tones

When twilight falls, the colors blend,
Crickets chirp their nightly send.
Stars twinkle like giggles in the dark,
As owls deliver their wise remark.

The shadows stretch with a comical yawn,
As nightingales serenade the dawn.
With every chirp, a chuckle rings,
Keep laughter alive through the night's flings!

Moths flit about in a laughable glide,
Dancing with fireflies, side by side.
The woods are alive, a joyous parade,
With echoes of laughter that never fade.

In this tapestry woven with twilight's charms,
The world whispers softly while holding our arms.
Together we dream, in the night's sparkling throne,
Under a blanket of laughs, we're never alone.

## Stories Held in Bark

In the park where trees do stand,
Lies a tale so grand and planned.
Squirrels gossip, tails on high,
While the branches wave goodbye.

Beetles dance and sing in glee,
Sharing secrets, bustling spree.
Roots whisper tales so profound,
Of lost acorns, never found.

The leaves chuckle with a breeze,
As they shimmy 'round with ease.
Their laughter rings from trunk to sky,
While rabbits hop and nearby pry.

Oh, the stories that trees tell,
Of critter drama, love, and yell.
In their knotted arms they keep,
A library of dreams, so deep.

## **Undercurrents of Elysian Green**

In the thicket, where critters plot,
Greenest schemes, oh, what a lot!
Frogs wearing crowns, they take the stage,
Singing songs of wise old age.

Dancing shadows, a card game's hot,
Ants with jokes, far from the lot.
Grasshoppers leap, they play their part,
While birds discuss the next fine art.

The crickets talk, their voices rise,
To serenade the starry skies.
Trees nod gently, their limbs in cheer,
For every giggle they overhear.

In this patch, where laughter thrives,
Every rustle, a tale that drives.
With every branch and every leaf,
Nature's jesters provide relief.

## The Voice of the Verdant Heart

Whispers flow from deep inside,
Where the branches stretch and hide.
Bumblebees with plump cheeks hum,
Sharing secrets, oh so fun!

Chirping birds with tales absurd,
Outsmarted by a clever bird.
Frogs who think they're Shakespeare's crew,
Pondering lines, quite out of view.

The thorns nod in rhythmic cheer,
As leaves debate on what to wear.
'Should it be bright or dull today?'
Nature's fashion, oh, come what may!

Roots intertwine with laughs and quirks,
Poking fun at all the works.
In every gust and playful swing,
Lives the essence of the spring.

## The Myth of the Whispering Woods

Once in woods, there lived a sprite,
Who made shadows dance at night.
With leaves for hats and sticks for swords,
They held council with the birds.

A rumor spread through bouncy boughs,
That squirrels dance and take their bows.
Hiding nuts was just a ruse,
To put on shows in forest hues.

Owl, the judge, sat proud and wise,
While raccoons stole the prize.
Every twist, each clever turn,
Left timbered hearts with joy to burn.

Humorous tales from night till dawn,
In the wood where laughter's drawn.
So gather close, bring your mirth,
For in this grove, there's endless worth.

## The Song of Inner Wilds

In the forest, a party of ants,
Wearing hats made of leaves, doing a dance.
They waltz with the beetles, they tango with flies,
No one knows why, but they're all in disguise.

The owls hoot a tune on the branches up high,
While squirrels play checkers, and kittens nearby.
A raccoon juggles acorns, what skill, what finesse,
It's a wild little circus, no need to impress.

A fox in a top hat narrates the grand ball,
While rabbits are moonwalking, they're having a ball.
The music from mushrooms adds flair to the scene,
As frogs leap in rhythm, their legs looking keen.

Beneath the bright stars, the night's full of cheer,
Nature's own party; it's the best of the year.
They sing for the moon, a weird, wacky crew,
In this wild little world, you're invited too!

## Odes to the Earth's Guardians

A hedgehog in glasses reads books on a stump,
While critters debate which nut makes a thump.
The badger plays drums on an old rusty tin,
And raccoons serve punch, it's a bash to begin.

Wise tortoises teach moves that are slow and profound,
How to groove with the grass, sway round and round.
While geese honk a chorus, a coyote adds flair,
With jazz paws he dances without any care.

In a circle of mushrooms, they spin and they twirl,
A beaver does ballet, giving nature a whirl.
The trees sway together, they sway, not alone,
While critters in costumes abound in their zone.

Each creature a guardian, with laughs echoing wide,
In a world full of antics, where joy doesn't hide.
When the night finally ends, they all take their seats,
For there's nothing quite like this to wrap up their feats.

## Constellations Beneath the Trees

Beneath the tall branches, the crickets convene,
They gossip like grandmas, if you know what I mean.
A deer in a poncho gives fashion advice,
While raccoons discuss how to roll in the spice.

The stars, they are twinkling, a light show deluxe,
While owls serve popcorn, they're clever, no bucks!
The fireflies flicker, they're not just for show,
They form constellations, oh look, now it glows!

With shadows and whispers, the night gets quite bold,
A skunk tells a joke that never gets old.
They laugh 'til they snort, under moonlit delight,
In the realm of wild fun, they dance through the night.

Each creature a neighbor, a friend wildly dear,
Guardians of laughter, so full of good cheer.
As dawn begins creeping, they sigh with no stress,
In this land of the wild, they're all truly blessed.

## **Vibrations of the Gentle Wind**

The breeze tickles leaves, what a whimsical play,
While bushes gossip secrets they whisper all day.
A snail in a tuxedo moves slow with great pride,
And critters applaud each new creature that glides.

A squirrel tosses acorns, practicing for shows,
With moves that are slick, everyone just well knows.
They cheer for the dance of the breeze through the trees,
As laughter erupts from the twirl of a bee.

Then frogs start a chorus, a funny old tune,
With grace that is charming, under the bright moon.
The wind carries giggles, oh what a tailwind,
As creatures unite, all their laughter they blend.

So let the leaves flutter, let the music ignite,
In this whimsical world, where all things feel right.
With friends in the forest, take joy to distend,
For laughter and fun never truly will end.

www.ingramcontent.com/pod-product-compliance
Lightning Source LLC
Chambersburg PA
CBHW071847160426
43209CB00003B/455